A PRAIRIE BOY'S SUMMER

A PRAIRIE BOY'S SUMMER

Paintings and Story by William Kurelek

TUNDRA BOOKS OF MONTREAL

The original paintings of *A Prairie Boy's Summer* are on extended loan to the Art Gallery of Windsor, Windsor, Ontario, Canada, from the collections of Hiram Walker & Sons Ltd., Walkerville, Ontario, Canada.

Printing history
1975 First printing, Tundra Books of Montreal
     US edition, Houghton-Mifflin
     Second Canadian printing
     A *New York Times* Outstanding Book of the Year
1976 UK edition, William Collins Sons
     Showcase Book Award
     Canadian Association of Children's Librarians Best Illustrated Book
     IODE Book of the Year
1977 Chosen by Toronto Public Libraries as one of the Top 100 Canadian Children's Books
1978 Norwegian combined edition, *A Prairie Boy's Winter and Summer,*
        Den Norske Bokklubben
     Canadian combined edition, *A Prairie Boy's Winter and Summer,*
        Tundra Books of Montreal
     Third Canadian printing
1979 First Canadian paperback edition
     Library edition
     Swedish, Danish, Finnish, Greenlandic and Dutch editions;
     German combined edition, *A Prairie Boy's Winter and Summer,*
        Otto Maier Verlag
1984 Second Canadian paperback edition
1988 Third Canadian paperback edition

ISBN 0-88776-058-9 (Hardcover edition)
ISBN 0-88776-116-X (Paperback edition)

Published in Canada by
Tundra Books of Montreal
Montreal, Quebec H3G 1R4

Canadian Cataloguing in Publication Data: Kurelek, William, 1927-1977.
A prairie boy's summer. I. Title. ND249.K87A317 971.2'0022'2 C75-9069-3

Printed in Hong Kong by South China Printing Co.

With love for my sister Nancy

Who more than anyone else shared with me the surprise and wonder
of prairie seasons as a child

Who has added to that surprise and wonder a sense of awe and love for
the Creator of those wonders. Many call it the Living Whole —
Ultimate Cause — Nature. We two call it: God

A PRAIRIE BOY'S SUMMER

1. Practicing for Field Day

In June, which Westerners regard as the beginning of summer, school was drawing to a close. William half regretted it, for summer always meant a lot of farm work, a lot more than in winter. At school there were three play recesses. True, it was also exam time; but he was always top of his class and the teacher sometimes even let him do his studying out in the grass by his lonesome.

One thing about June that William didn't look forward to was the last day of school — field day — when his school got together with two others in the district to decide which of the three would win The Shield that year for athletic strength and skill. In the last two weeks, training for it got really serious, and the teacher took time off to direct and record her pupils' progress.

There was no way to hide the fact kids even younger than William could run faster and jump farther and higher than he could. So he preferred the novelty races like the sack race, the three-legged race or the wheelbarrow race. He even liked the undignified peanut race in which the contestants had to get down on all fours and push a peanut along the ground with their noses. But William had one consolation. His school rivals during the rest of the year were now on his side. He knew they wanted him to do well in the competitions so The Shield could be won for their school.

2. Softball

In June it seemed to William they played baseball at school every day. He wasn't as quick or strong as the other boys his age so he didn't care for baseball. He preferred less competitive games like "bat er-up" or "21 and in." But when sides were chosen for baseball even the small kids had to play, because there were seldom more than 25 children in the one-room school. A softball, about twice the size of a hardball, was used, and even though it was softer, it still stung William's hands, especially when it was new.

William offered to play an unimportant position like second base or midfield. He stood there and daydreamed of making a sensational catch that would gain the respect and admiration of the others. Suddenly he had to snap back to reality for someone had hit the ball and it was high in the air heading toward midfield. The opposing team yelled "Miss it! Miss it!" There were even catcalls to rile him! "Butterfingers! You can't catch!" He ran under the ball and made a flying leap with arms outstretched. The sun was in his eyes. So do you think he caught it?

3. School Lunch under the Woodpile

In winter the children had to eat their sometimes frozen sandwiches at their school desks. But in summer they had a bigger choice of lunch places. One of the boys' favorite spots was under the school woodpile. It offered just the right amount of shade if the day was hot, and it cut down the wind that tugged at their lunch wrapping.

William was a fussy eater and wasn't always excited about the contents of the black metal lunch box he shared with John. He always seemed to be getting peanut butter, which stuck to the roof of his mouth. Or corn syrup. Or homemade jam which had soaked right through the bread by lunchtime. Or hard-boiled eggs that choked him. Or else the butter was too thick. Baloney was all right if the bread hadn't been soaked with French mustard. Milk from a thermos helped the sandwiches go down. He was fond of dessert but he didn't get it often.

William preferred the fancy sandwiches — like brown sugar and butter — that came out of the lard pails and brown paper bags of his poorer neighbors and sometimes he persuaded them to swap. Once in a long while a wonderful smell rose out of his lunch box when it was opened, and he knew he was in for a treat. Real British Columbia apples which his father occasionally bought on his trips to town for the mail and farm supplies.

4. The Field Day

William couldn't escape it. The last day of school — field day — came. If his school was competing at one of the other schools, they were driven there in the back of a farm truck. The officials were usually teachers and school trustees, and competition was by age or sex or grade. A starting line was made in the grass with lime, and the finish line was a tightly held string. All toes were on the line as the official called out "One for the money. Two for the show. Three to get ready. And four to GO!" Away they went. William could see the backs of the fast runners pulling away from him. If he heard some slower unfortunate clomping along behind, he took comfort.

A lot of parents came and there was a picnic in the shade behind the school. The jumping and novelty races came after lunch. Winners earned points for their school and money for themselves: 15 cents for first place, 10 cents for second and 5 cents for third. Losers, like William, had to bring money from home to spend in the confection booth which had been built out of poplar branches against the outside wall of the school barn.

At the wheelbarrow race William heard someone shout: "Hey, look at that pair out front. The barrow's being carried! He's just pretending to touch the ground. Disqualify them!"

The day ended with two baseball games. If a school won both games it usually took The Shield because a ball game was worth the most points. William's school won it most often because it had the most pupils. It didn't seem exactly fair.

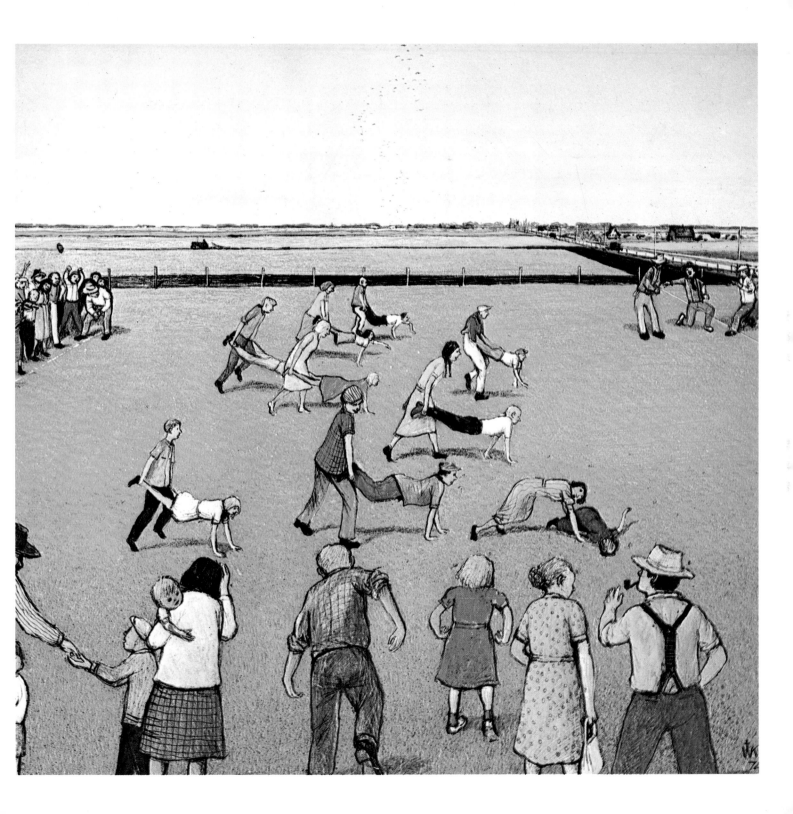

5. Swallows Dive-bombing the Cat

The first cat they had on the farm was called simply "Kitka" which is Ukrainian for cat.

William remembered her playing around the stove when she was only a kitten. She produced many litters in the seven years that she lived. Seven is a ripe old age for a farm cat, so she had a special warm spot in the family's heart, and was tolerated in the farmhouse. All the other cats had to live in the barn.

When Kitka saw William's mother leaving for the barn at milking time she'd set out ahead, knowing there'd soon be fresh warm milk.

However Kitka had enemies there — barn swallows. Their nests were half cones of mud glued to the sides of beams, close to the ceiling. A cat hadn't the slightest chance of getting a swallow unless a baby fell to the floor, but the swallows, William was amused to note, hated even the sight of a cat. When Kitka was still a good way off in the yard the swallows would begin dive-bombing her. Wheeling into formation high in the air, they'd zoom down to within a foot of her head, and scream rude swallow words into her ears. Kitka's tail would twitch angrily but she kept right on her course, pretending not to notice. She was plotting nonetheless, for once in a while she'd make a leap into the air and try to paw one of the bombers to the ground. She never succeeded, because they were too fast for her.

Meanwhile John, Winnie and William were at the barn door riling up the cows so they'd drop their droppings before going into the barn. But they must not be made too nervous or they would withhold their milk.

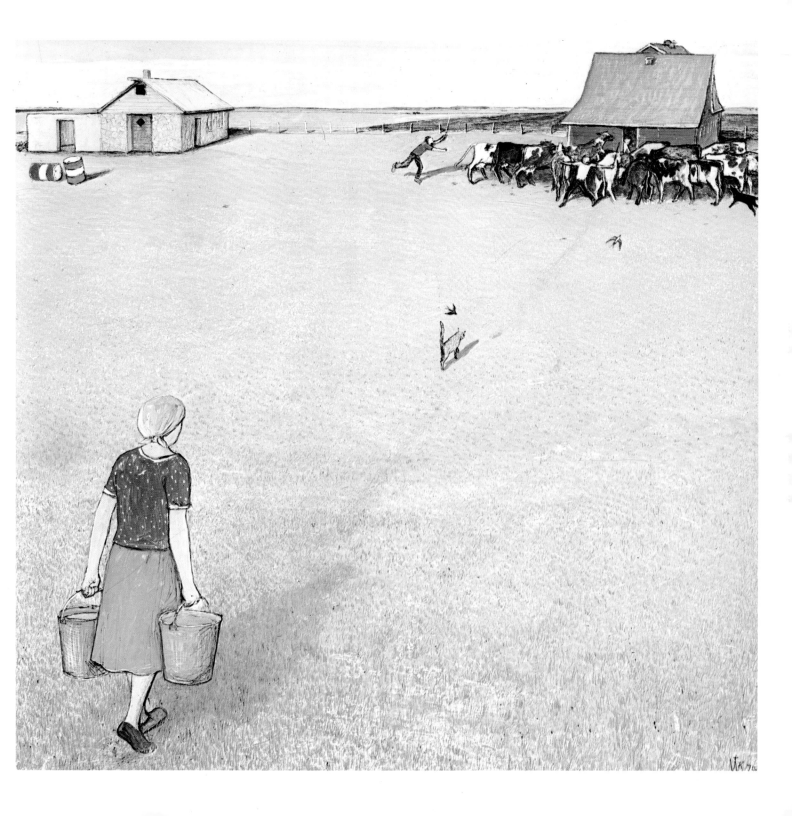

6. Catching Baby Killdeer

William and John loved birds. So when they were sent to fetch the herd at milking time they made sure the cows didn't step on a killdeer's nest they knew of near the barn road. A killdeer's nest lies flat, naked and exposed on the ground, and this one was so cleverly camouflaged that William had found it only by accident. One day as he was passing the mother bird flew up, then fell to the ground some yards away, crying and fluttering, pretending her wing was broken. He knew from the extra-big fuss she made he must be very close to her nest.

On this particular evening the herd scared the mother bird up again and William was delighted to see that the eggs had hatched! Darling fluffy little bits of life, standing high on legs thinner than toothpicks, scattered in all directions. Not yet able to fly they tripped on blades of grass and William caught one easily. He could feel the teeny heart going pit-a-pat in his hand. He knelt there trying to soothe it by stroking and talking. "Please, I'm not going to hurt you. I just want to hold you for a minute." How he wished he could tell the frantic mother that he wouldn't dream of harming her babies.

"Hey, get those cows in!" His mother shouted from the garden where she was hoeing out the weeds in the cabbages. William let the bird go, knowing it would reunite with its family at the nest when he had gone and they felt safe again.

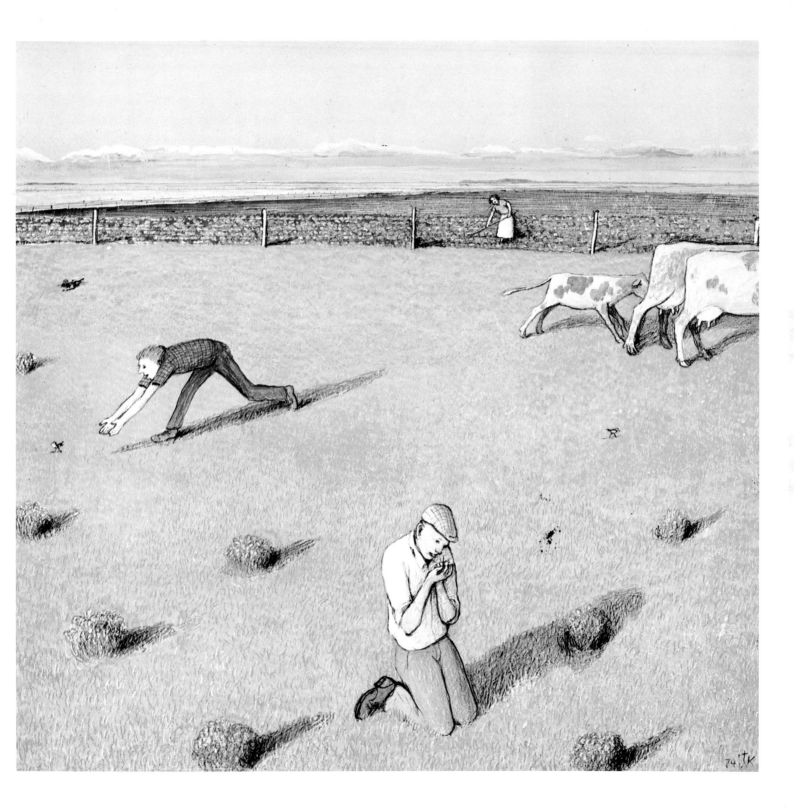

7. Pasturing Cows

Before his father could afford to put an electric fence around his temporary pastures, William often had to look after the cows all day. This wasn't a bad job if the cows were satisfied and if the farm dog stayed with him to help, because then he could read a pulp Western novel Steve lent him at school and daydream he was a cowboy of the American frontier.

But faraway fields always look greener to a cow, and even when the pasture offered enough to eat, the herd sometimes got restless. William swore they plotted their escape, for they pretended to graze as they moved right up to a grain or cornfield. Then, in less time than it took him to read another line and find out if his hero had escaped the ambush, there they were in the forbidden field.

Sometimes William tried an ambush of his own to teach the cows a lesson. He'd hide at the edge of the cornfield, and as soon as he heard the clicking of ankles and snortlike breathing of the grazing herd, he'd let fly with his slingshot at the lead cow. Once he struck her between the eyes with a pebble and she raised her head in the air and shook it about as if dazed. William panicked. Had he permanently injured her? What would his parents say? To his relief she soon rejoined the retreating herd. But half an hour later the lesson wore off, and the herd was once more edging its way back to the cornfield.

8. Burning Quack Grass and Harrowing

During the hot dry days of summer William got to know other Western weeds besides the ones often found in the garden. This season between sowing and harvest was the time to summer fallow — to work the land that was resting from bearing crops.

First, the field was plowed to bury the grasses and weeds so that they would die and turn into a kind of fertilizer. Then harrows, discs or spring-tooth cultivators were used to pull out any weeds that survived the plowing. These were left for the hot sun and wind to dry out.

The toughest weed to kill was called "quack grass" or "couch grass." Its roots were long and stringlike and they caught onto the soil even though they were torn out and lying on the surface. If there was enough moisture the quack grass put out both roots and green shoots and, if you left them alone long enough, they soon formed a whole colony or patch in the field. Quack grass roots had to be raked or harrowed together and burned. It was a tiring, dusty job walking after the harrows all day and William's shoulder ached from lifting each section when its spikes got clogged with roots.

Stacking and burning the piles of roots left by the harrow was more fun. William made a game of this. Although he had a box of matches in his pocket, he tried to avoid using them by carrying fire on his pitchfork from one pile to another. He had to run to get it across in time — but not so fast that his speed blew the fire out.

In the distance William could see clumps of bushes quivering and floating as if in a vast lake. This was a heat mirage, and the little whirlwinds that sprang up now and then in the field had an odd Ukrainian name: "a devil's wedding."

9. Haying

Haying was an important early summer job on dairy farms. When his father went into dairying William had to learn the many steps necessary to make a haystack out of a field of grass.

William's father planted his own grass, unlike his neighbors who rented sections of the bog to the east and cut natural grass. William envied the neighbors' boys for they sometimes stayed out on the bog for two whole weeks, cooking out in the open and sleeping under the wagon just like gypsies. He could see their stacker machine throwing hay up onto huge stacks on the horizon. William's father didn't have one, so their stacks were handbuilt and low.

The mower was the first machine used in haying, and it had to be oiled often. Its steady clatter made William sleepy, and only near accidents — like almost cutting a frog in half with the blade — kept him awake. In wet years there were lots of frogs. William liked the smell of fresh-mown hay, but he didn't like the job of raking the dried hay into bundles, first one way, then the other.

The next step, called sweeping, William was not allowed to do, because John had tried it one day and had an accident. The sweeper was like a giant comb on wheels between two horses. It pushed the hay bundles to the center of the field so that a stack could be built there. The horses were jittery because of horseflies and had to wear wire baskets to protect their tender noses. John's horses bolted from the horseflies, pulling the sweeper with its load of hay so fast that it overturned and rode over him. Only the hay into which he fell saved him.

William had to learn to build the stack right and at the same time catch more bundles of hay thrown up to him by his father and mother. Once they left a stack of clover unfinished and an approaching thunderstorm that night forced them to get up at 2 a.m. to put a peak on the stack. They saved the stack but not themselves from the downpour. Tired and sleepy and looking like drowned rats they got back to the house at dawn.

10. Thunderstorm Approaching

William loved the excitement of a thunderstorm during the day. It usually came
in the afternoon after a hot sultry morning. This day his mother had been watching
the dark cloud form and begin its swift approach. She yelled to the children,
"Go round and close all the doors in the yard! Get the poultry in!" She was raising
turkeys as well as geese and chickens that year. Turkeys are not as stupid as
chickens and can be herded easier. Winnie and William went after them.

The dark sky cracked open with a crooked dagger of lightning. William instinctively
drew in his neck; he knew that when a storm was that close, the thunderclap would
follow hard on the flash. It came — WHOMP! The earth seemed to tremble from the
crash. He liked the after-rumble, as the echo resounded between earth and heaven.

It was only at night that thunderstorms really frightened him. On the prairies
they sometimes lasted all night. Even though the house had lightning rods he didn't
trust them to keep the lightning from setting fire to the house.

Of course he knew the farm safety rule about not standing under a tree for shelter.
Yet when he was working in the fields, it was a big temptation to avoid a soaking
by heading for the clump of very tall trees in the field across the road. William had
actually been hit by lightning once when he was closing a gate during the first few
drops of rain. Fortunately it wasn't too big a jolt for it had already traveled a mile
down the barbed-wire fence. William dropped the gate and ran.

11. Corn Cultivating

In the district where William grew up, dairy farmers raised corn for ensilage. The livestock ate the stalk, not the cob, so the farmers grew a special hybrid corn that produced little or no cob. This corn had to be cut while still green and chopped up into the silo or ensilage hole before it had dried all out. It would then ferment from its own moisture and weight.

But even early in the summer, when it was only a foot high, the corn needed special attention. It had to be hilled and weeded. William's father bought a new cultivator and after he himself had learned to work it, he put William on it. William didn't like working on farm machines because the monotony put him to sleep. But he had to be alert on this job; if his shoe slipped on one of the two foot levers he'd find to his dismay the shovels below were digging up corn instead of weeds.

After a while William got good at the job and he could let himself daydream a little. His father had promised him that when he passed grade nine he and John would go to a high school in the big city. One of his daydreams was of being surrounded by city high school students who listened in admiration to his stories of farm adventures.

How mistaken his daydreams turned out to be! The city boys weren't interested in nature and didn't care to hear his stories. Many years would pass before William found a way to get people interested.

12. Milking Time

Milking was a job William didn't look forward to, especially on hot, fly-filled days.

Outside there might be a blue sky and perhaps a refreshing breeze, but inside, the barn was like a furnace. To get at the teats on the far side of the cow's udder he had to lean tight against the cow's belly, which heaved and radiated heat like a big oven. Adding to the discomfort of the sweat, flies used his head and hands as a landing field. William had to be ready to grab the pail of milk away in case the cow kicked at a fly and put her foot in the pail. She used her tail as a fly swatter, too; and its coarse, dirty hairs often slapped William right across the back of the neck. He'd spray the cow with flytox, but its effect soon wore off. It was best when his little sister Nancy held the tail.

As relief from the milking ordeal, William amused himself by squirting one of the barn cats that waited nearby, meowing for its evening ration. It would jump away as if upset, but really it liked the white shower; for it sat down further off and set about licking away the milk.

If William's mother — who was the best milker in the family — was away for some reason it meant he and John had ten cows each to milk. That night their wrists would ache so badly they couldn't sleep. Everybody was relieved when the family became prosperous enough to buy a set of milking machines.

13. The Swimming Hole

William, like many another prairie boy, never saw a large body of water till his midteens. He did have a place to swim though, after the older boys of the district widened the bog ditch to the east of his father's farm in one spot. They built a sod dam and even a rough diving platform. It was the neighborhood swimming hole from that summer on.

There was no sand on the bottom, only clay and mud. The boys could feel it squishing up between their toes but they couldn't see it because as soon as they jumped in, they raised clouds of sediment that made the water opaque as pea soup. William didn't dare open his eyes underwater. By late afternoon, when it was time to head home for milking, the cloud had flowed as far as the first bridge.

Two kinds of water creatures lived at either end of the swimming hole and William disliked them both. Black catfish with their peculiar whiskers hung around out of curiosity at the clear upper end, and the dam at the lower end was like an apartment for dozens of crayfish. William hated the thought of stepping on a crayfish but couldn't resist raising the sod once in a while to stare at them. Sometimes as a joke a crayfish or a frog would be put in a swimmer's shoe. Another trick was to hide a swimmer's clothes. This was rather mean because they all swam stark naked and the victim was left with nothing to wear home.

No one brought towels. After their swim, they ran around in the big field opposite the hole. When sun and wind had dried them, their bodies were covered with a fine, white coat of clay which they brushed off. Nobody lived way out on the bog, but they still had to keep one quarter of an eye open, for once in a rare while a gang of local girls would visit the bog on their bikes.

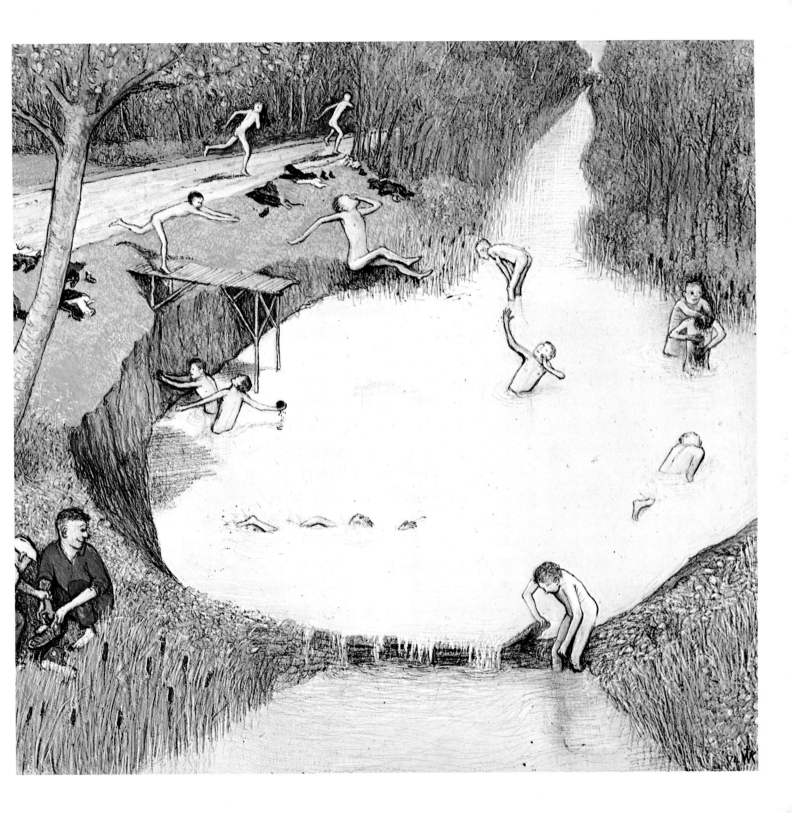

14. Making a Smudge

Apart from milking, dairying was much easier in summer than in winter. After his father put up an electric fence the cows took little looking after; all the boys had to do was pump a tankful of water for them.

But every summer evening, there was one more favor the cattle appreciated — especially in wetter years. Clouds of mosquitoes appeared — people said they came off the bog to the east — and William's parents would send him out at sunset to build a smudge fire to protect the animals from the pests.

Making a smudge wasn't the same as making a bonfire though it was sometimes called that. William's father showed him how to mix layers of dry straw with layers of wet straw or manure so that the pile would glow and smoke instead of blaze. Otherwise the fire would burn out long before daylight and the cattle would be unprotected. Of course, if there was no breeze the smoke didn't help much, for it went straight up. But that didn't happen very often.

William found there were really no gentlemen in the animal world. Even if the cows got to the smudge first, the farm horses always came along and took away the best places in the smoke. The cows knew the horses were bullies, so they moved out of the way before they were bitten or pushed aside.

15. Plowing

Plowing was a long, lonely job. On the old tractor William didn't fall asleep so easily because its steel wheels made for a rough ride. But the new tractor had rubber tires and there was only the noise of its two cylinders to keep him awake. "Bach, bach — bach, bach" its exhaust repeated over and over all day long and even after supper till it was completely dark. As long as William could still make out the furrow he had to keep plowing.

William's father adjusted the plow levers to the right depth, and because the tractor was new it hardly ever broke down. The only excuse for stopping was when Nancy brought out some water or lunch. Or if the fuel was low. William didn't dare turn off the motor because he didn't have the knack of turning the flywheel to start it up again. One time, after trying for two hours and getting blisters all over his hands, he had to go out on the bog to fetch his friend Billie to help him.

Nor was William strong enough to tip the fuel barrel to fill the fuel can with distillate. This was a cheaper, less refined fuel than gasoline and was used only in tractors. Sometimes he siphoned it by sucking on the end of the hose, but occasionally he got a mouthful of it and didn't like the taste. Another way he got the siphon going was to insert the hose into the barrel, holding his hand tight over the other end. Then he would pull the hose out and down very quickly. If he was lucky the fuel would start to flow itself.

Making turns on the tractor was easy enough after the first year of bungling. William also got the knack of pulling the trip rope to raise the plow when he reached the end of a furrow or to drop it after making the "E" turn. A flock of gulls followed him as he plowed to gobble up the worms and bugs the plow turned up.

16. Cutting Grain

William was only twelve when his father drafted him and John into harvest work.
He might have had another year or two to grow stronger and more capable if
the war hadn't come and taken away all his father's hired hands. Another sign of the
war was the bombers that began to appear in the sky from the direction of the city
airfield. They practiced dropping their bombs far out on the bog to the east and then
they circled back over the farm toward the city.

At first William was put on the old black tractor, which pulled two binders. His father
rode on the front one, John on the second. The old binders broke down a lot,
so William had to be ready to make a quick stop when his father yelled "Whoa!"
To make up for time lost repairing equipment, they had to cut grain well into
the night, even after the moon rose. William and John were so dead tired they fell
into bed without even washing off the field dust.

The second year was easier. By then the old tractor had broken down completely
and his father bought a new, bright green one. Now they had time to look around
and enjoy watching prairie animal life. As a patch of grain still uncut in the
middle of the field grew smaller and smaller all kinds of creatures ran out —
partridges, gophers, rabbits, skunks. The farm dog was always on hand, hopeful
for game, but he hardly ever caught anything. Rabbits ran too fast, and he had
learned by painful experience not to get too close to a skunk.

Nancy was just strong enough that year to carry water out to the workers in the field.
They appreciated it, for cutting grain was hot, dry work.

17. Stooking

Some years there were wet spells even during harvest time. It wouldn't actually rain — just turn foggy and drizzly, but too much moisture wasn't good for the grain. Wet grain, or grain that had sprouted, was good only for cattle feed. Gray weather made William sad.

If the grain was too wet to cut, the family could still stook for a while. William's mother was a good stooker and taught him how to do it properly. You picked up two sheaves, held them either by the binder twine or under your arm and then brought them down firmly to the ground with their tops together, leaning against each other. Another two pairs of sheaves brought down in the same way, on either side of the first two, completed the stook. A stook was shaped like a teepee so the rain would run off it, and it had a hole in the middle so the wind could dry it inside.

When stooking, everyone wore long sleeves and, if possible, trousers and even gloves to protect himself from stubble and straw scratches. William hated barley because the sheaves were small and sometimes fell apart, and their beards scratched his face. The thing he dreaded most was getting a barley beard in his mouth or throat. It irritated like anything and it took some fishing with his fingers to get it out.

In wet years there were also more mice than usual. They had to be killed because of all the grain they would eat. William and his mother heard John yell "A mouse!" and saw him chase after it. The mouse might succeed in hiding in the next row of sheaves, but it got caught when that row was being stooked.

18. Mending Pigs' Fence

It seemed that a large part of William's life on the farm was spent capturing escapees. Horses, bulls, chickens, calves, pigs — all had their "prison breaks." Pigs caused William the most trouble. Because they are such notorious wanderers, they were penned inside a page-wire fence. But they are also notorious rooters so every few days they'd dig under the fence and escape, heading for parts unknown. When William finally found them, it was hard to herd them back. Eventually, of course, most escapees got hungry and came back to be fed.

But the family had a faster way to get the pigs back — as long as at least one pig was left in the pen. William's father would twist its leg or ear, and it would squeal loud and long. A pig's hearing is very sharp, and soon William would see the whole herd come charging back from the other end of the farm to defend their brother in distress. As soon as they rushed in through the open gate or through the hole they'd dug, the innocent one would be released from his tortures.

Then William and John had the job of repairing the fence. While the boys worked, the pigs stood at a distance in the weeds, sniffing and snorting and watching with their mischievous little eyes. "Look at them," said William. "I bet they're figuring how to undo this repair job!"

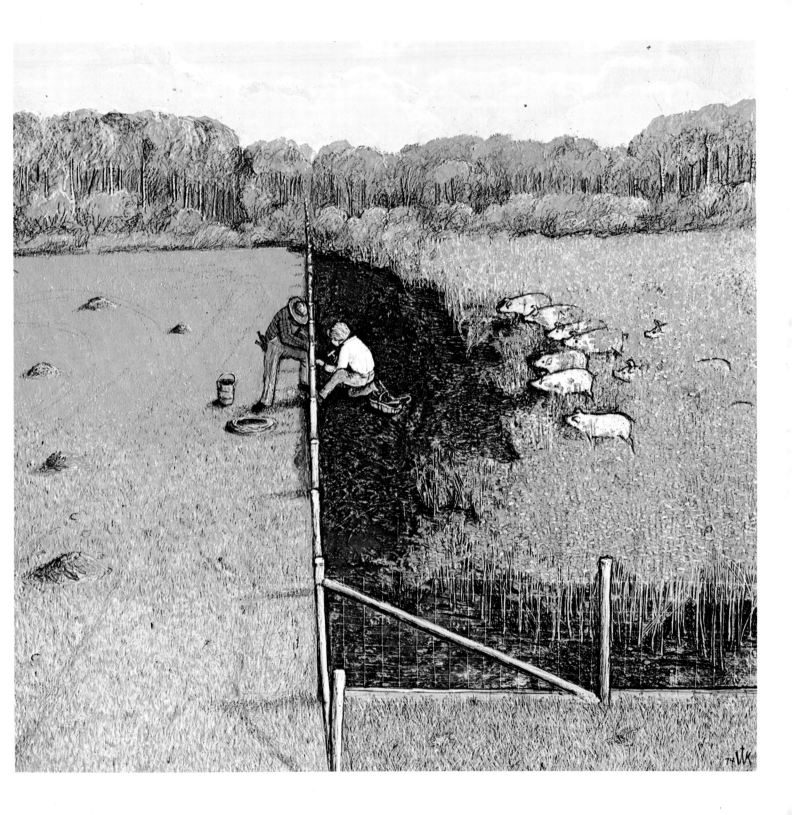

19. Gopher Hunting

School always opened on the first of September. All through the summer holidays the schoolhouse seemed to sleep, as if resting from the beating the kids had given it the last school year, and gathering strength for the new one in the fall. Weeds managed to grow high in front of the school buildings, and out in the tall grass gophers dug their burrows. Gophers are pests to farmers. When there were too many of them the municipality even paid kids a one-cent-a-tail bounty for them.

When the boys returned to school, they kept their eyes open for gophers and as soon as they spotted one they formed a hunting posse. Some had stones and clubs. Others carried pails of water. Often a dog from a nearby farm joined the chase. A gopher usually escaped the first pail of water poured down the hole by emerging from a second, backdoor hole. "There she goes!" yelled William as she scampered to another hole. They had to act fast then, for they knew that the gopher realized she was in danger of drowning and would quickly build a dam below ground. The boys always knew if she succeeded because only a little water went in before the hole was full. But if bubbles came up they knew they had her. She'd surface, wet and miserable, and try to escape by running between the legs of the attackers to still another hole. William sometimes felt a twinge of pity for her. But a pest is a pest. Blinded and confused she'd run around in circles under a rain of stones, sticks and clubbings until someone made a direct hit and finished her off.

20. Bows and Arrows

Threshing time was a sure sign autumn was taking over after summer. Already there was a certain chill in the air at night. From the schoolyard William could see bright new straw stacks rising here and there on the horizon. His father's were the most numerous, for he still prided himself on being a grain farmer. A threshing scene is exciting even at a distance. William felt a little guilty enjoying his recess when it was the busiest season for his parents on the farm. But he knew they excused him, for his father thought education even more important than farm work.

William enjoyed his recesses more than usual the year he was twelve because the other boys had gone along with a new sport he introduced — archery. William had a natural knack for carving and his bows and arrows were the best for distance and accuracy. At last, here was a sport in which he excelled.

William had read about a way of using the feet to shoot. So they all sat down to try it, and sure enough it worked. The arrows went clear out of the schoolyard into the pasture on the other side of the highway. It seemed the boys were conquering the awesomeness of the prairie expanses at last.

In another two years William too would be leaving the grassy schoolyard — for the concrete and cinders of a city high school playground.

When William Kurelek died in November 1977 at the age of 50, he was Canada's best-known painter. The four books he had created for children were received with equal enthusiasm by adults and honored with 22 major national and international awards.

His fame continues to spread. His books have been published in the United States, the United Kingdom, Australia, Germany and Austria, Denmark, Finland, Holland and Greenland. In Norway, a 70,000 one-volume edition of A PRAIRIE BOY'S WINTER and A PRAIRIE BOY'S SUMMER made him almost as well known as in his native Canada. In Sweden where six of his books have been published, the winter and summer PRAIRIE books have been particularly popular. Each was issued in a 50,000 paperback edition for the school children in that country. LUMBERJACK, his account of his years spent cutting wood in northern camps to earn money for his art studies, has also received a long string of honors. Another book published during his lifetime that has touched more and more people with the passing of time is A NORTHERN NATIVITY, his magnificent retelling of the Christmas story; its reading along with slide shows has become an annual event in many churches.

Since his death two additional books have been published by Tundra: FOX MYKYTA, the great Ukrainian folk tale which he illustrated with 72 drawings, and THE POLISH CANADIANS, his series of paintings of the early struggles and courage of that immigrant group. His ambition was to paint the history of all of Canada's varied peoples. He succeeded in leaving his vision of the Inuit, French-Canadians, Irish, Ukrainians, and Poles, as well as of Christians and Jews. A retrospective of his paintings has been touring Canada over the past three years.